T0137498

Robyn Besemann knows her audience—women who long for a meaningful, purposeful life who want to grow stronger in confidence, biblical strength, and courage. If that describes you, I encourage you to get a group of women together and study this book together. Robyn reminds all of us that we can grow beyond our uncertainties and complacency, and become women who stand strongly in God's truth, bold faith and steadfast joy.

Carol Kent, Speaker and Author
Becoming a Woman of Influence (Nav Press)

Robyn does a great job in the analogy of standing in hard places without a strong spiritual walking with our Lord. From taking baby steps in baby shoes all the way through growing in the Lord and standing in adult shoes. She reminisces about wearing her mom's high heels as a little girl and how it was to walk in those heels as a little girl just like it's hard to walk in an adult's shoes without strong relationship with our Lord. Even as adults we walk on rocky ground and we need to be strong in our spiritual journey as we stand on the rock in heels.

Linda Ranson Jacobs
Author, Consultant
Program Developer for DivorceCare for Kids

Standing on the Rock in Heels

Discovering Your Spiritual Stride in Biblical Shoe Fashion

Robyn Besemann

WESTBOW
PRESS®
A DIVISION OF THOMAS NELSON
& ZONDERVAN

WestBow Press books may be ordered through booksellers or by contacting:

WestBow Press
A Division of Thomas Nelson & Zondervan
1663 Liberty Drive
Bloomington, IN 47403
www.westbowpress.com
1 (866) 928-1240

THE HOLY BIBLE, NEW INTERNATIONAL VERSION®, NIV® Copyright © 1973, 1978, 1984, 2011 by Biblica, Inc.® Used by permission. All rights reserved worldwide.

ISBN: 978-1-9736-7876-2 (sc)
ISBN: 978-1-9736-7877-9 (e)

Library of Congress Control Number: 2019918174

Print information available on the last page.

WestBow Press rev. date: 2/11/2020

Acknowledgments

I give all glory to the God who created me and gave me the gifts and talents He did. I am forever grateful for the ministries He has called me to lead since I was a young woman. I will serve Him and will strive to bring hurting people to His healing arms until I go to be with Him.

I am grateful for my late parents, Rev. Darrel and Phyllis Bellville, for raising me in a loving home that was filled with joy, purpose, and living with the principles of the Word of God. My upbringing set me up for a vibrant life of ministry, so I say, "Thank you, Mom and Dad. I carry your legacy."

I thank the Lord for my husband, Ivan for supporting me in many ways, as I walk in ministry. He has always encouraged me and shown great patience as I try to do what the Lord leads me to do. The day he said, "I will never stand in front of what God calls you to do", is the day I found freedom to serve with my whole heart. "I love you with all my heart, Babe."

I am grateful to the six women who so graciously proofread "Standing on the Rock in Heels." They were so faithful to look at every word, be honest with their thoughts and opinions, and prayed over what I wrote. Thanks to Kathleen Wilson, Lynda Hodge, Terri Labarbra, Donna Norvell, Joyce Young, and Linda Oliver. "Thanks, Ladies. You are such a blessing!"

Lastly, I thank our home church, First Baptist Church of Eugene, OR for all the support they have given me throughout my years of ministry there. This is a church family who has encouraged, prayed for Robyn B Ministries, and shown their love in endless ways.

Contents

Foreword

Robyn has written a message that we can understand and apply to ourselves. Fun, yet practical, this book is designed to touch the heart of a woman and give sound principles for a healthy spiritual life.

"What type of spiritual shoes are you wearing today?" the book asks. In one day I may wear two or three pairs of shoes. Heels for church, flip flops to water my outside plants, and slippers to make me cozy. My life is complicated, and so is yours. We have so many roles, that we sometimes get too busy and forget to center our lives on Christ.

We, too, as Christians, go through different stages. Happy, sad, depressed, concerned, yet it's sometimes difficult for us to understand that through all our seasons and challenges. God is more powerful than anything we face, and we can always rely on Him. The more we balance ourselves on His Word, the better we can keep sound footing and run a successful race. Robyn writes, "It's hard for us to comprehend sometimes when we forget where we put our keys on any given day." That's why we need to seek God, stay in His Word, and do all of the practical, doable steps she suggests to lead victorious, exciting lives in our Savior. Read this book and get started. You'll be glad you did! Walk out your faith, ladies. That's what our God called us to do.

Marilyn Rhoads
Oregon Christian Writers President

Introduction

Do you like shoes? Do you delightfully wander through a shoe store, drooling at the various styles of footwear on the shelves? Maybe you can't go on a shopping trip without coming home with a new pair. If you are like me, you can relate to all of this. Now I can't wear the type of heels I used to, but I sure can admire them on someone else, and usually the girlfriend wearing them is much younger than I am. Can I get a witness?!

Now I realize there are many women who couldn't care less about buying new shoes, except when it is truly necessary, and going into a shoe store or department can send them over the edge, but hopefully, you will find a great deal to encourage you in this book anyway.

I like the saying, "A woman can never have enough shoes." Amen, sister! I like tennies, sandals, pumps, boots, stilettos, and almost every other type of shoe in between. The only stipulation for me is that they are cute and have some bling or unique feature on them somewhere. "Life is short, so wear cute shoes."

Our walk with God should be the core of who we are. In Joshua 22:5, he is talking to some people and says, "Love the Lord your God, walk in all His ways, obey His commands, hold fast to Him and serve Him with all your heart and all your soul." In Psalm 89:15, David says, "Blessed are those who have learned to acclaim You, who walk in the light of Your presence, O Lord."

When I began to prepare for a women's retreat speaking engagement, I was given the scripture theme, Joshua 1:6–10. It says:

> Be strong and courageous, because you will lead these
> people to inherit the land I swore to their forefathers to

give them. Be strong and very courageous. Be careful to obey all the laws my servant Moses gave you; do not turn from it to the right or to the left, that you may be successful wherever you go. Do not let this Book of the Law depart from your mouth; meditate on it day and night, so that you may be careful to do everything written in it; then you will be prosperous and successful. Have I not commanded you? Be strong and courageous. Do not be terrified; do not be discouraged, for the Lord your God will be with you wherever you go.

I began to wonder what retreat theme could come out of these verses, so I pondered for a couple of days. On the third day, after praying again, it became clear—"Standing on the Rock in Heels." "Perfect! Thank You, Lord God!"

My mind began to flood with different types of shoes and how they could relate to our spiritual walk with God, so we can become strong and courageous. It seemed like there was no end, and I couldn't wait to get started developing the notes for the retreat!

I began to think back (waaaaay back) when I was a little girl and how, as a pastor's family, we didn't have much money, so my shoes were often hand-me-downs from my older sister or from people in our church. They didn't always look that great, but at least I had shoes.

I remember when my dad would use a can of black shoe polish on those worn shoes and buff them so they were nice and shiny for church. I also remember when my white shoes would get almost too old to wear, and my dad would apply white shoe polish to cover the cracks and worn spots, and I would proudly wear them to church for a little while longer.

I loved my mother's high heels and liked to try them on and attempt to walk in them. She liked shoes with little straps, and to this day, I am still drawn to strappy heels. I always thought she looked like a fancy lady in them, along with her hose and her pretty dresses. My Aunt Meryl, from California, would wear those black stiletto "Barbie shoes," with the one strap over the toes, and wear her full-length fur coat. She looked like a movie star, and I loved to be near her.

When I got into my midschool and high school years, I began to keep up with the latest fashions, which included clogs, platform shoes, and other chunky footwear. So much for the feminine look, huh? Oh well, that would come later when I became a "lady" like my mom.

Of course, shoes aren't just for looks, although that is the first thing we may notice. They have a function—to cover our feet, to protect them, and to help us to walk confidently without fear of injury.

This is where this book begins. We will compare several types of shoes with different types of spiritual walks. It will be an interesting exploration of shoes as they relate to sturdiness, support, confidence, walking boldly, commitment, and a growing faith, as well as the pitfalls that can trip us up. So put on your cute shoes, and let's go for a walk!

Chapter 1
Baby Steps

When we first ask the Lord into our lives, we are like newborn babies. Many of us remember our baby's first steps. Those little chubby legs, adorable plump feet, and "piggy toes" just make us love them even more, don't they? One day, after learning to crawl all over the house, they decide to try to pull themselves up and hold onto a chair or a table. They fall back on their puffy-diapered bottom, and it isn't long before they try again. Once they master that trick, they step their little foot out, put weight on it, and usually fall down again. Up again.

Down again, up again, etc.

The day finally comes when our toddler lets go of the table or chair and tries to move forward. Usually, we are not too far in front of them, calling their name and encouraging them to come to us on their own two feet. More falls, more attempts, and then they take their first real step! What a triumphant moment that is!

Once babies get their legs under them, so to speak, then you can't stop them, right? They have a new freedom. Then the only thing children wear out faster than shoes are their parents! *Isn't that the truth?*

After that first step, they still fall and get hurt and cry and fuss, but they get right back up and try again. They become more determined with every new step.

Isn't that like us as new Christians? We are babies who are just learning to use our spiritual legs. We are unsteady, unsure, and unprepared for what is going on and what is ahead. We fall and get hurt, we cry and we fuss, and we need help to continue on in this thing called Christianity.

We don't know the songs, the books of the Bible, or what's in them. We don't know what is right and wrong in some areas, or even know much about who God is, besides what we learned as kids. Maybe we weren't raised in a religious home at all, never went to church, and now have no idea what the rules are.

It is always a delight in our *Chained No More¹* classes when someone asks basic questions like, "How do you know that God loves me?" or "Who are Mary and Martha?" They are still baby Christians and have a hunger for God's truth. We were all there once, right?

Some of us live like Christians on Sunday and then take off our spiritual shoes for the rest of the week. Maybe we are satisfied with that and think we are doing the right thing by only being a good person.

Many of us have lived a life full of trauma and crises, and the damage is great. We use that as a filter through which to look at life. Our filter may be anger, depression, low self-worth, fear of rejection, or feelings of abandonment or betrayal. We always feel like we are on the outside looking in. Walking into a church is a huge stretch for us because we don't feel we fit in. We are spiritually walking barefoot.

Jamie (a fictitious name) was a forty-three-year-old woman who, according to a first glance, lived a very hard life. Some of her teeth were missing, her clothes were tattered, and her long hair covered her face as she hung her head. She had a long story of abuse, neglect, prostitution, incarceration, drug and alcohol addictions, and numerous suicide attempts. Her attitude about life was horribly tainted, and she felt everyone was against her, especially Christians. She didn't feel worthy, but for some reason she decided to reach out and try to find God. Her first stop was a *Chained No More* class in our church. She walked into that first class with fear and trembling. Truthfully, we as leaders were a little nervous too as she entered the room.

Her thinking and speaking were chaotic as she tried to answer deep personal questions in our class. She was welcomed with open arms by our leaders and our participants, and it was unnerving to her. Jamie had a very difficult time with trust, so she didn't trust the good words that

---

¹ Robyn Besemann, *Chained No More: A Journey of Healing for Adult Children of Divorce/ Childhood Brokenness* (WestBow Press, 2011).

surrounded her that day. But each week she came in, she would try to assess what the right answers were as she tried to fit into the group. She began to feel comfortable to ask questions about basic Christian beliefs, although still with some skepticism.

Five weeks into the *Chained No More* process, she began to sit up straighter, fix her hair, look people in the eyes, and dress a little neater. We began to notice the changes and compliment her. She told me, "I have never felt such love in my life! I can feel it as I come into the room each week!" God's love was surrounding and covering her, which was such an unfamiliar experience for her.

One week, she told us she was getting new teeth. Years of abuse and addictions had ruined her mouth, and she always tried to hide it by covering her mouth when she smiled or laughed. The next week, she came in the room with her smile shining brightly and announced, "I got my new teeth!" We all applauded and hugged her because we knew the significance this had for her. She no longer felt like an outsider. Praise His name!

By the end of the thirteen weeks of *Chained No More,* Jamie began to define herself by who God said she was and not what anyone or anything had ever told her. She was free from the chains that had burdened her. She began to realize her true worth. She got a couple of jobs, helped in our church ministries, found a better apartment, reconnected with her estranged son, and had some medical procedures done to improve her health. She was stepping out in her spiritual shoes in a big way! Praise God!

You see, just like Jaime, we can be very uncertain and afraid to take that first step into a church, class, or small group. Even walking into the sanctuary for the first time can be overwhelming. We as church congregants should always be on the lookout for these new people who walk into our churches each week. We can come alongside them, guide them to where they need to go, sit with them during the service, start conversations, and be the extensions of Jesus's arms to them, can't we?

Some of us have been Christians for a while, or even most of our lives, but have never really grown out of our spiritual baby shoes. Maybe we go to church on Christmas, Easter, or Mother's Day with Mom. Maybe we don't feel pretty enough, clean enough, smart enough, or perfect enough, so we go as seldom as we can, if at all. We might be the ones who fill up the back row. If we stay at this spiritual level, we can never be all God created us to be. It is like buying a car and then only driving it to the store and back once a month. There could be so much more benefit from that car if we would use it more often and keep it well maintained.

> Then we will no longer be infants tossed back and forth by the waves, and blown here and there by every wind of teaching and by the cunning and craftiness of men in their deceitful scheming. Instead, speaking the truth in love, we will in all things grow up into Him who is the Head, that is, Christ. From Him the whole body joined and held together by every supporting ligament grows and builds itself up in love, as each part does its work. (Ephesians 4:14–16)

This world is full of false teaching that is contrary to the Word of God. Human dreams, visions, good works, goals of financial prosperity, and special prayers happen in such a way that we as mere human beings believe we may have more power than God intended.

After all, we deserve God's grace, don't we? *No!* We deserve nothing from the Almighty God; it is merely by His grace, mercy, and unconditional love that He blesses us.

When we as baby Christians step into the Christian world, we see that if we do this and do that we will have the Lord's favor, but when our lives do not improve or remain the same, we assume God's favor is not for us and is built on performance and not grace.

Where did you come from? Did you have a childhood filled with the chains of divorce, abuse, neglect, abandonment, foster parents, adoption, etc.? Maybe you have absolutely no idea what real love is all about, and now the church is asking you to trust in God's love for you. Many people struggle with this.

Shelly grew up in a family where her father was an elder in the church and was well respected by the congregation but was horribly abusive at home. The church didn't know that as soon as they got home, she and her siblings were at the mercy of their monster of a dad, yet every Sunday they would all file into the church looking like the perfect family.

Shelly grew up not knowing the slightest thing about God's love or even what human love was supposed to be. She heard about His love every Sunday, but she never felt it. She never felt she was good enough for God's love because she wasn't shown love by her own earthly father. She was very educated in biblical studies and was involved in ministries as she tried to earn God's love by serving. She thought that God's love was performance based, so she just kept trying. That is contrary to what God's unconditional love is all about. She learned how to hide her feelings, be a people pleaser, and strive for approval, and in her marriage, love was subjective.

> Love is patient, love is kind. It does not envy, it does not boast, it is not proud. It is not rude, it is not self-seeking, it is not easily angered, it keeps no record of wrongs. Love does not delight in evil, but rejoices with the truth. It always protects, always trusts, always hopes, always perseveres. Love never fails. (1 Corinthians 13:4–8)

Now, does that sound like the love you grew up with? Did you feel valued, treasured, and nurtured by your parents? Maybe you took what you were given, and if you weren't raised in an atmosphere of unconditional love, it is no wonder you are stuck in your spiritual baby shoes or even walking barefoot. If you were not raised in the church, you may not see the benefit of growing in your faith and building a community of believers.

If we have been betrayed and deeply wounded, chances are that trust is a big issue. If we were never taught about Jesus, or we had authority figures in our lives who caused traumatic wounds, it is no wonder trusting even the Lord God can be a struggle.

The truth is that you are an adult now and this is *your* life. *You* make the decisions. *You* can walk away from all the faulty thinking you have had because of someone else. *You* can dig into God's Word and find truth about His love for you and who He made you to be. How does that sound?

You know, if you really think about it, your first spiritual baby steps could be a testimony of how someone accepted you and began to disciple you step-by-step in your walk with Jesus, just like Jamie. Who was that? A neighbor, client, coworker, Sunday school leader, friend? So now, what is the next step?

When we grew to be a toddler, one day our mom put us in sturdier shoes, like the old Striderite ones. Do you remember those? They had hard soles, were white, and came up to our ankles. They weren't very fashionable, but at that age, it didn't matter. What made them cuter was if we had ruffled socks to dress them up, right?!

Wearing these sturdy shoes allowed us to feel more confident and maybe even venture out to try the stairs or walk on the sidewalk holding our parent's hand. These shoes made it much easier to walk with more support, due to sturdier soles.

This reminds me of when we begin to get stronger in our walk with the Lord. Just like our parents helped us walk, people come alongside us in our spiritual walk to help us as we move forward in our faith. These people may include a pastor, small group leader, or mentor, etc.

They may have supported us by meeting consistently, attending Bible studies or counseling sessions, or by just walking alongside of us daily.

Spiritual baby steps translate into learning the truth of who we are by:

- Learning God's promises and believing them
- Putting feet to our prayers (actions)
- Listening to the Holy Spirit's voice and putting feet to what He is convicting us to do
- Nurturing ourselves spiritually and personally
- Recognizing and ignoring the enemy's jabs, in the name of Jesus
- Living and loving like Jesus and extending His arms to others
- Getting back up every time we fall, in order to keep going
- Learning to live a life of gratefulness and living in His joy and freedom

As we grew older, we were allowed to choose our own shoe fashion and show the world who we were. Just like we make choices on what type of shoes we want to wear, we choose the kind of walk we have with Jesus.

Sometimes, trauma and crisis can determine our spiritual footwear for a certain amount of time. We may have to wear waders to walk through the deep waters of depression, and that can last for years. It is just merely surviving and is a means of protection and not drowning. We may have to wear running shoes to try and keep up with everyone's expectations of us. Sometimes our own expectations are too high. If we look deep, there are many reasons why we live under that pressure.

We may wear spiritual slippers (more on this in the next chapter) for a long period of time because we feel safe and protected in them. We rarely wear them outside and don't care if we wear them out or not; we are comfortable. Spiritually, we can get so complacent and noncommittal that we never grow in the Lord at all, and life goes on as always.

Sometimes, our shoes don't fit, and we can develop blisters, like challenges in our life. There is too much pressure and friction, and we are unable to have peace in our souls. We may try to fix those personal blisters by using bandages of alcohol, drugs, or food, or by just keeping busy but never getting to the root of our dismay.

Sometimes, we go barefoot and sink into the quicksand of depression or great anger, and we can't take another step because we are indeed frozen in our crisis. Even the smallest pebble of a struggle can hurt and cause us to not move forward. Maybe we have tried counseling, self-help books, or medications but have not found answers or relief.

The questions to ask before reading any further are: What type of spiritual shoes are you wearing today? Are you content in comfortable shoes or would you like to step out in a new pair of spiritual footwear? Are your spiritual shoes too tight? Do you live by too many rules, rituals, and expectations? Do you need more freedom to be all God made you to be? Do you even *know* who He made you to be?

For the past forty years of ministry, my passion has always been to "help people see who God says they are and not what anyone or anything has ever told them." That is why I have written this book, and that is why I am so glad you have chosen to read *Standing on the Rock in Heels.*

Blessed are those who have learned to acclaim You, who
walk in the light of Your presence, O Lord. They rejoice
in Your name all day long; they exult Your righteousness.
For You are their glory and strength. (Psalm 89:15–17)

When it gets right down to it, your walk with God is just between you and Him. He loves you right where you are this very minute. If you just sat there and breathed, He would love you just the same. He knows you and loves you and wants you to have a richer walk with Him, step by step. He wants you to move past the spiritual booties and dance in His glory and freedom like never before in magnificent spiritual shoes.

Chapter 2
Bunny Slipper Belief

Do you have a pair of favorite slippers? You know, the ones you have had for years that are worn out, maybe smell a little funky, and that you would never wear even to the grocery store? Maybe they are slippers you were given as a gift, or maybe you bought them yourself. Whenever you walk into the house, you slip them on, put your feet up, and sometimes just have to say, "Ahhh."

I was in a store recently and took a look at the slipper selection there. I was amazed at the many types there were! There were pink slippers for little princesses, blue ones for little robots or train conductors. There were funky ones for teens with bright colors, cartoon characters, and rock bands. There were solid brown or black ones for men with fur, corduroy, and tweed.

Then I moved to the women's section of slippers and was surprised to see the many different styles there. Some of them looked comfortable and some of them not so much. There were soft, cozy ones, ones with little heels and feathers, some with bows and buckles, and some just plain and practical. Choices. Choices. Choices.

Sometimes we can get so complacent in our spiritual life that we would rather not step out of our comfy spiritual slippers. We don't have to try anything new. We don't care if we are worn out or "smell bad," and life is just what it is.

What we don't realize is that when we become spiritually stagnant and lazy, we drift further and further from God and live in our own ways instead of His. We may stop going to church, reading God's Word, and communicating with Him, and therefore may become blended into the deterioration of our country and our world, and sink into hopelessness.

If we don't believe that God is in control and always has been and have complete faith in Him, the media alone could bring us into depression, anger, and unbelief.

"What kind of a God would let all of this suffering happen in our world?"

"If He doesn't care about our world, how could He possibly care about me and what I am going through?

"Why does He cause hurricanes and tornadoes and tsunamis to wipe out entire towns and kill hundreds or thousands at a time?"

Eventually, we sit in our spiritual slippers and let the world go by. They are comfortable and safe and make no demands on us.

Listen to what it says in Hebrews 6:10:

> God is not unjust; He will not forget your work and the love you have shown Him as you have helped His people and continue to help them. We want each of you to show this same diligence to the very end, in order to make your hope sure. We do not want you to become lazy, but to imitate those who through faith and patience inherit what has been promised.

Now, let's look at some of the reasons we may become satisfied with living in our spiritual bunny slippers:

- Maybe we didn't have a strong upbringing in spiritual things. Maybe our parents didn't go or just sent us on the church bus while they stayed home. We didn't see commitment to growing in things of God, so it doesn't really cross our minds very often.
- Maybe our upbringing included being in church every single time the doors were open, and we just got tired of it. Maybe, after all these years, we don't think there is much we haven't heard already, and "we're fine."
- Maybe we were abused by the church in our past, and we refuse to get caught up in religion again. Many people have become

disillusioned by churches that manipulate verbally, and sometimes physically abuse members, as well as use guilt and shame to bring members to their knees in submission or financially bully them.

- Maybe we are just lazy after a full week of our working schedule, or we feel it is just "too much work" to get everybody dressed and out the door to attend church. Let's see … What would happen if we just stopped eating because it was too much work to fix a meal for our families? We would become malnourished and eventually die. The same goes for our spiritual lives, doesn't it? Think about it.

- Maybe we have gotten to the place where we are older now and have served in the church for many years, and "they just don't need me anymore." Well, there is always a great need for the wisdom of those who have experience in things of God. You may not do the exact same thing in serving in the church, but you certainly can support those who are. Genuine words of encouragement are priceless! Do you remember what that meant to you?

There are many reasons why we can sink into our spiritual slippers and let the world pass us by. It is very easy to spiritually slow down when we don't attend a church where we are growing, isn't it? Now I am not saying that the church is the end-all, but statistics show church attendance is at an all-time low, and there are many reasons for that. Our county in Oregon is the least-churched county in the United States—not something to brag about, by any means. Looking around at our society, we can see the deterioration of our world and how far we have strayed from God's principles and guidelines.

Decades ago, the local church served as a social network, an educational place of growing and learning, a support system, a place of hope and joy, and a beacon in the community. What happened? It mostly functioned as a family, with purpose and love.

My father was a pastor, and back in the day, the church building was our second home. We built strong relationships with members and attendees. We rejoiced with each other, mourned with each other, raised families together, served our community and each other, worshipped together, learned God's Word, and encouraged one another. We didn't shy away from joining a church family, because we saw the importance of connecting through the blood of Christ. We were committed members, moving forward in our community together. This is the experience that my family had when I was growing up. I am so grateful for the legacy of family and faith I grew up with, and the result of that is part of this book.

There was a time, in my early twenties, when I put on my own spiritual bunny slippers and walked away from the church. Since I grew up in a church and our entire family life revolved around it, I wanted to see what else was out there. I decided that I would try bars, go dancing, and see how the world lived. What I saw was so foreign and offensive to my spirit that it wasn't too long before I realized I missed the atmosphere of the church, of a church family, and things of God. I am truly grateful that the enemy didn't take hold of me so much that I suffered trauma in those months. I took off my spiritual bunny slippers and came back to God—praise His name—and I never looked back!

These days, with fewer but bigger churches, it is almost impossible to gather the entire congregation together as a family to worship. We have satellite churches, sister churches, home churches, and online congregations. Many churches have resorted to "small groups" or "life groups," where a small circle of people meet in homes during the week, study the Word, and build relationships. The purpose of these groups is to serve to bring the entire congregation closer together, to serve together, and to worship together in a community.

Commitment these days is almost a dirty word. Authority is too. There are no absolutes and, therefore, even the Word of God is suspect. We interpret the Bible by our own experiences and personal interpretation. The problem with that is that we can interpret through our own human filters—filters such as anger, hurt, depression, abuse, low self-worth, fear, etc.

Here is an example: "Behold I am with you always ..." For someone who has been abandoned and betrayed, they can read that and say, "Yeah, riiiight. That's what my dad said too before he left our family destitute and shattered." Trust has been broken in the majority of people today—through shattered families, broken relationships, poor business dealings, or abuse they have suffered. It takes a lot of time and a supernatural moving of the Holy Spirit for them to be able to surrender unbelief, mistrust, and their whole self to the Lord God. Do you see why it would just be easier to sit back in spiritual slippers instead of doing the work to make it work?

Another area of just almost giving up in our slippers is when families have been divided, so some family members may go to church and some may not. Many times, parents and children (especially teens) go to different churches each week, so they don't even have unity in what should be the most important element of their families.

The breakup of a family through divorce presents another challenge; children cannot attend consistently because they travel back and forth from parent to parent in their court-ordered "parent plan." Many times children live through so much chaos during the week that they are unable to sit still in Sunday school; they cannot focus their minds to memorize scripture, and they have a distorted view of authority of any kind. After all, from their perspective, adults in their lives have devastated them and their families.

> If we want to build our church membership today, and if we want to preserve the church of the future, we need to look at where our communities are and what kinds of families are in our communities. It is not about programs or gimmicks. It is about families. It is about relationships. It is about reaching out and sharing the love of Christ to a new and different generation in a culturally diverse and ever-changing world. (Linda Ranson-Jacobs, *Attract Families to Your Church and Keep Them Coming Back*, Abington Press, 2014)

Whatever the reason, are you feeling very comfortable in your spiritual bunny slippers? Does it just seem safer to isolate and not get involved in a church family? Is it time to get out of your spiritual lounge chair and become less of a spiritual couch potato?

Of course there are times to sit back, rest, restore, and build your strength back up. Maybe you got too involved and are feeling burned out. Maybe you have gone through a crisis and need to "get your feet under you" a bit. Maybe you realized that you were giving out a great deal more than you were spiritually bringing into your life, and you need to reprioritize. If you feel the Holy Spirit "reeling you back a little," listen to Him and put on your spiritual slippers for a bit, but don't let them get funky and worn out. Find a personal Bible study to help you spiritually grow and strengthen your walk with Jesus Christ.

Ladies, let's step it up and take that first step toward a stronger and more vibrant walk with Jesus. It might be uncomfortable at first. Beginning new habits usually are. Begin by:

- Asking God to give you a passion for Him and His Word.
- Reading a portion of scripture that speaks to you. Maybe even memorize it.
- Finding a friend who you respect and meet for coffee. Talk about your desire to become more of who God wants you to be and how this could happen.
- Talking to the women's ministries leader, a pastor at a local church, or maybe a spiritual mentor who will disciple you to a stronger walk with Jesus.
- Getting involved in your church and/or community a little at a time, as you feel more confident.

Kick those spiritual bunny slippers off once and for all; put on some stronger spiritual shoes, stand up straight, shoulders back, and move forward step by step, beginning today.

Chapter 3
Flip-Flop Faith

Flip-flops are all the rage these days, especially in warmer climates. Those few pieces of rubber have made quite an impact on fashion, but they are older than you may think. Flip-flops have actually been around for at least six thousand years! You can see primitive shoes in rock paintings dating from the Stone Age period, some fifteen thousand years ago. And we thought Old Navy came up with them!

The oldest surviving examples of thongs were made from papyrus and palm leaves in 1500 BC. Other countries that had this type of footwear were African made with rawhide, and East Indians made wooden sandals. China and Japan made ones with rice straw, and Mexico made theirs with the yucca plant. Some of those don't sound like they would be comfortable to walk in, do they?

In researching the subject of thongs—something I didn't think I would ever need to do—I discovered that in the Middle East, different cultures made different sandals by putting a strap around a different toe to identify where they were from. To tell you the truth, I am not one who likes straps between any of my toes, so I would not have liked these at all, no matter which toe they had a strap around!

Looking at America, the first flip-flops came after World War II when our soldiers brought back the Japanese *geta*, a kind of sandal with an elevated wooden base. Of course, we needed to try and improve them, and they ended up being made in California in many bright colors soon after the war.

Even though we don't call them thongs anymore, we have almost made a fashion culture out of flip-flops. They can cost anywhere from $1.50 to hundreds of dollars for those blinged out with Swarovski crystals. More than two hundred million pairs of flip-flops are now sold in our country every single year. That's a lot of rubber on our American feet!

Let's look at the reasons for their popularity and compare them with what I call "flip-flop faith." The first reason so many flip-flops are sold is because of how comfortable they are. We can easily slip them on and wear them with almost anything, and we hardly know they are on our feet. Some brides wear white ones on their wedding day, for heaven's sake! One thing that is not beneficial about this footwear is that they don't have a shank, so they give minimal support. They may be cute, but they don't have much strength behind them.

Looking at flip-flop faith, we can really see the similarities. Flip-flop faith is a casual kind of faith that comes and goes. Yes, we have accepted Jesus into our lives and that's about it. We go to church whenever. We read God's Word whenever. We spend time in concentrated prayer whenever, and that is mostly when we are asking for something. We just kind of "slop around" in our faith, and again, there is very little support. This kind of faith is similar to bunny slipper belief, isn't it? Flip-flop faith can make it so we hardly know we are a child of God, and neither does anyone else. Hmmmmm.

First John 1:6–7 says:

> If we claim to have fellowship with Him, yet walk in the darkness, we lie and do not live by the truth, But if we walk in the light, we have fellowship with one another and the blood of Jesus, His Son, purifies us from all sin.

The second reason flip-flops are so popular is because they are usually cheap. After all, they are usually a few pieces of rubber or plastic and cost very little. When you wear them out, you just throw them away and don't feel guilty, right?

The spiritual application to this type of cheap faith is that it includes little commitment at all. There is no sacrifice and no involvement, to speak of. When being noncommittal, we let others do all the work in the church, and we just take. We get a cup of coffee, go into the service, listen to the music and the sermon, and then walk out to the parking lot and go to lunch.

Many times, however, people with flip-flop faith do most of the complaining in a church because their needs aren't being met, but they also don't get involved and serve. Because of no commitment, we don't build support and fellowship with other believers. We can just "take off our faith" and forget about it. We kick off our spiritual flip-flops and never grow deeper than that. Sometimes we walk away from God too and dispose of our spiritual life. We all have dips in our commitment to Christ and need to rededicate our lives to Him after falling away so that our relationship with Him is close, strong, and growing.

There are many reasons why church attendance is down in America, and here are a few of them, according to *Huffington Post*:

- Demographic remapping of America. The race ratio is changing. Do our political beliefs prevent us from reaching out to all?
- Technology. Instead of embracing technology, we are not connecting with the younger generation. This generation lives on smartphones, texting, Instagram, and Facebook. Are we connecting with them? Or do we merely say, "I just don't do technology."
- Leadership Crisis. Clergy abuse, affairs in the church and the cover-ups, and high percentages of clergy addicted to pornography. Fundamental preachers and congregations have been driving people away from the church faster than any other issues combined! The enemy is alive and well in the church. Can I get an "amen"?!
- Competition. People have more choices on weekends than simply going to church.

Another reason why our American churches are losing the battle is because of religious pluralism—so many different types and denominations of churches. Battles about traditional or contemporary worship styles splits churches wide open instead of bringing us together in praise. Many feel that there is phony advertising for churches. We say everyone is welcome—except for those who are not a traditional, straight family and, like the rest of us, sitting in the pews.

Remember the scripture about how "man looks on the outward appearance, but God looks at the heart"? (1 Samuel 16:7). Let's jump to Ephesians 5:1–2: "Be ye imitators of Christ as dearly loved children and live a life of love, just as Christ loved us and gave Himself up for us as a fragrant offering and sacrifice to God." Do you see the connection? If we are being imitators of Christ, we will care more about the heart of others than we do what they look like—an amazing goal for the believers in and outside of the church.

How can we, as a church, be a safe and a caring place as we extend the arms of Jesus to those outside our church doors every Sunday? How can we encourage people to have more than merely a flip-flop faith?

Looking at flip-flop faith, have you stopped going to church and meeting with other believers? Ask yourself how that happened. Was it gradual, or was it complacency that happened over time?

When did you stop reading His Word for direction, inspiration, and growth? Did you perhaps find self-help books more helpful for the issues you have? Was it just easier to read some other flawed human being's perception and ideas than it was to read the Truth of the Word of God? Think about it.

Have you fallen into flip-flop faith by neglecting the Lord altogether and not communicating with Him? Praying is just talking to the Lord God—sharing your true feelings and thoughts, seeking Him for answers, and praising Him for who He is. Let Him hear your heart and what lies deep within you. He loves you and wants to have a lasting and rich relationship with you.

Maybe you have been going through a big crisis, and you are mad at Him for allowing it to happen. Tell Him. Do you question His very existence? He knows that, and He still loves you. Maybe you have given your life to Him and are trying to live a life He would want you to, but have questions of how to do that. Maybe you need to seek His will for your life in some decisions, such as the right job, the right spouse, or the right church to attend. You might be filled with shame and guilt from things in your past, and you don't think He would want to hear from you. Oh, but He does! If you are a parent, what could your own child possibly do to make you stop loving him or her? Nothing, right? That is just human love, so you can imagine the deep, perfect, and unconditional love God has for you.

He knows everything, but He wants to hear from you so you can build a closer relationship with Him.

> Come to Me, all you who are weary and burdened, and I will give you rest. (Matthew 11:28)

> Do not be anxious about anything, but in everything by prayer and petition, with thanksgiving, present your requests to God, and the peace of God, which transcends all understanding will guard your hearts and your minds in Christ Jesus. (Philippians 4:6–7)

The third reason why many of us buy flip-flops is because of the endless variety of colors and styles of them. There are plain ones, sturdy ones, blingy ones, some with heels (most without), some fuzzy, some made out of rubber, and some out of leather. There is just no end to the choices, right?

On the spiritual side of such variety, we see that many times we look around at what other beliefs are, and we may dabble in them. We read book after book, watch YouTube/TV pastors and evangelists. So what happens when there are differences in beliefs on the pages of books or on the television screen? Do we research to find out our own beliefs, just scratch our heads and say, "Oh, well," or do we go to God's Word to see what He has to say?

How do you get solidity in your beliefs? Do you expect the pastors, rabbis, and priests to do all the work, or do you seek out truth for yourself? Does walking with God mean you compare or try to fit in with Christians or people at church?

Maybe if you say the right "Christianese," dress the right way, and sing the popular worship songs, then you will be a solid Christian? Do you go to church and just walk away, or do you carry what you learned with you the rest of the week? Do you indeed have flip-flop faith?

When we get a new pair of flip-flops or any other shoe, we enjoy looking at our feet while we walk in them. It's all new. This is kind of like when we first become a Christian. We are excited; we feel good, and all is right with the world. There! We did it! We are going to Heaven and that's that. Now, we can live how we want to, right? *Not!*

When we accept Christ, we become His child, and His Spirit dwells in us. With that comes the fruit of the Spirit, as you are transformed. The following scripture spells out what that transformation includes.

> The fruit of the Spirit is love, joy, peace, patience, kindness, goodness, faithfulness, gentleness, and self-control. (Galatians 5:22–23)

But if we have flip-flop faith, without growth and fellowship with other believers, the soles begin to wear thin, and pretty soon something sharp can bring injury. We decide not to wear this old pair anymore and begin looking for a new pair. You can't really put new soles on cheap flip-flops, so, therefore, they become disposable, just like our walk of faith can become old and stagnant. Soon, we don't even remember those old flip-flops or our spiritual life. We walk away, and life goes on.

Other things about flip-flop faith:

- Maybe we don't read His Word for several months.
- Maybe we only pray when we need something, like using God as a candy store.
- Maybe we go through all the actions or do the bare minimum, but our heart isn't engaged. We kind of just fit Him in.

So how do we go deeper in our spiritual life and grow stronger and more confident in who we are in Christ?

First of all, we need to be honest and recognize our need for a stronger spiritual shoe. There are endless Bible studies, DVD or online series, TV church shows, and books on Amazon.com to help us get a more solid footing in our walk with Jesus.

One sermon on Sunday is good, but we need to take responsibility for our own walk and relationship with Jesus. If we don't, we will not be able to withstand the enemy's attacks—kind of like when we may be wearing flip-flops and step on a nail!

Please believe me when I say that flip-flop faith is not enough. We need spiritual stability and strength to experience His joy and freedom to be all we were meant to be, so we are protected from the enemy's jabs.

James 1:2–4:

> Consider it pure joy, my brothers, whenever you face trials of many kinds, because you know that the testing of your faith develops perseverance. Perseverance must finish its work so that you may be mature and complete, not lacking anything.

Flip-flops are nice to wear for comfort but not for long periods of walking because they wear down and provide too little support for our feet. The next step is up to you as you continue to grow in your walk with Jesus. Are you ready to take stronger spiritual steps?

Chapter 4
Practical Pump Religion

I love bright, unique, and colorful shoes. I am drawn to strappy heels, like I mentioned before. The type of shoe I am the least attracted to are plain pumps. You know, those shoes that most women wear in the corporate world day after day with their suits, or the little old ladies wear with hose, while carrying their matching black handbag. I remember many grandmas wearing pumps to church every Sunday and the older they were, the lower the heel. I used to wear heels, but now I don't because of my own age and knee issues. I was never a Plain Jane type of shoe girl though. I liked sassy heels.

Pumps are one of the most popular styles of women's shoes today, and they are also one of the most difficult to define. Men used to wear them in the seventeenth century and called them "Pompes."

In their most basic form, pumps have closed backs and low-cut fronts down by the toes. They don't have laces, buckles, straps, or ties to keep them on, Pumps can, however, have all kinds of toes, such as peephole toes, closed box toes, pointed toes, etc. Pumps nowadays can be embellished with bows, straps, or small buckles and still look proper.

Unlike the flip-flops, pumps are steadier and conform around the foot for support. Toes don't stick out between little straps, and we can usually walk awhile in them, if they fit well. Professional women wear them every day to the office, but I am sure most women promptly take them off under the desk, and as soon as they can upon leaving the office.

On hot days, pumps can make our feet feel hot and cramped, but we persevere and wear them only as long as we have to. We can't really move our toes much around in them either, because our feet are so restricted. Pumps can protect our feet from hot sidewalks, rain, snow, or sharp rocks, so there are some positive things about these shoes.

Unlike the flip-flops, we can get new soles or heel tips put on pumps so we can wear them longer. We can polish them so they look nice and wear them to a variety of places and events. They are proper. They are *practical* pumps.

There are many similarities between these practical shoes and our walk with God. When we first accept the Lord, many times we set out to learn the rules and guidelines of what being a Christian is all about. We want to know where we fit in and feel accepted with this new group of people.

Here are some of the questions and concerns we may have:

- How many times should I go to church per week?
- Do I have to read the Bible and pray every day? Where do I begin?
- Do I have to speak in tongues?
- Which translation of the Bible should I read?
- Should I only listen to Christian music?
- Do I have to raise my hands during worship?
- How much money am I supposed to put in the offering? Is there a minimum?
- Am I going to the right church? How do I know?
- Should I stop reading anything but Christian books?
- Should I change the way I dress?
- How are Christians supposed to talk?

Do you see how complicated and uncertain this can be for a new believer? Some of us have come from religions that strongly rely on practical works, rituals, and traditions of the church. "To get this, you have to do this, and you have to do that." How can we possibly meet all expectations, and what do they have to do with "freedom in Christ"?

Many times, what this can do is make us think that God's love truly is conditional and performance-based, when quite the opposite is true. Here are some examples:

- If you say this prayer or do this church ritual, you will be in good standing with God.
- If you eat or drink this but not that, you will earn more "spiritual points."
- If you pray this way, God can hear you more and will answer your prayer.
- If you have a certain emotional experience, then you have the Spirit.

I remember years ago when I led LIFE Aerobics, a large regional gospel aerobics program, one of my students said to me, "I don't care if you *are* a Baptist. You, my dear, are filled with the Holy Spirit!" I was dumbfounded and replied, "Well, yes I am, and I was from the moment I accepted Jesus."

From the book *Search for Significance*, by Robert McGee, LifeWay Press:

> To meet our compelling needs for security, personal success, status, beauty, wealth and the approval of others, we drive ourselves to achieve, doing virtually anything to make people happy with us, and we spend countless hours and dollars trying to look or act "just right." Often we avoid situations and people where the risks of failure and rejection are high. It's a rat race that can't be won by simply running faster.

> We need to get off this hopeless treadmill and learn to apply the foundational truths that can motivate us to live for Christ rather than for the approval of other people. He has given us complete security and challenging purpose. These are not based on our abilities, but on His grace and the power of His Spirit.

Profound, Mr. McGee! In other words, God's love is not conditional; nor is it performance-based. It is given freely and filled with grace.

Well, let's begin to look at wearing spiritual practical pumps in the church. Pause for a moment to think what those might look like.

If you serve a certain amount of time on committees, boards, teach Sunday school, sing in the choir, lead a Bible study, or serve in other areas, then the Lord will love you more and reward you, right? Also, others will think you are wonderful.

You seem to do everything right and proper; you are serving in the church almost every evening, you go to church whenever the doors are open, and … *check, check, check*. On the surface, we are serving the Lord 100 percent and helping out in the church, but if explored, it can reveal something deeper.

A friend of mine worked in her church office and had her finger on the pulse of the entire church. She did an exceptionally good job of keeping track of all meetings and events, kept the pastor's calendar, did the bulletin, planned women's events, and ran herself ragged every Sunday, making sure everything ran like clockwork. That is what she was being paid for. But looking deeper, she began to understand why she worked so hard. She grew up feeling worthless, had to care for her siblings, didn't have a voice, and had to do everything with perfection, or there would be consequences.

Let me tell you something about perfection, because I know many people who struggle with that. There is a difference between perfectionism and striving for excellence. Many times, perfectionists have difficulty having close relationships because it seems no one can meet their expectations. It is difficult for them to accept constructive criticism or confrontation because of their past damage, so they can get defensive and fight to justify even the smallest of mistakes. Many times, perfectionists feel they need to control their world around them because they live in a world of fear of failure, not meeting expectations, and not being accepted. It is like a locked cage that they are unable to escape from, but they are fine as long as things are perfect in their eyes. Are you a perfectionist, and does any of this sound familiar?

Can you see the long-lasting results of a childhood of negative input and excessive expectations? These are more chains from our past that affect our adulthood that need to be explored and from which we need to be healed.

What good is it, my brothers, if a man claims to have faith but has no deeds … Faith by itself, if it is not accompanied by action, is dead … As the body without the spirit is dead, so faith without deeds is dead. (James 2:14, 17, 26)

These scriptures are sometimes taken out of context in an attempt to create a works-based system of righteousness, but that is contrary to many other scriptures. James is not saying our works make us righteous before God, but he is making it clear that genuine saving faith is *demonstrated* by good works. Works are not the *cause* of salvation; works are the *evidence* of salvation. It is also not about looking good (or perfect) to others.

Many times, on the other side of this is a disconnect with our intimate relationship with Jesus. We can get to the point of resentment because we are so tired from all the church activities we are involved with. Sometimes, we can become sort of a martyr because "I do all the work around here and nobody will help me, but … I love to serve the Lord anyway." Many times, if we are honest, if we are not pleased with what someone did, we either redo it or just not ask that person again and just do it ourselves, causing possible burnout. Are you that woman?

Here is a scenario to drive this home.

There is a notice in your bulletin that some volunteers are needed in the first grade Sunday school class. You have never really connected with elementary-aged children, and your plate is full with the missions committee, women's ministries committee, and on the team to hostess events. You attend two Bible studies, and you were just nominated to be a deaconess.

But … this notice in the bulletin is there. What should you do? Your kids and husband hardly ever see you as it is, and they have been telling you they miss you. You feel worn out, and you are beginning to feel taken advantage of, and feel torn between church and home. You are kind of afraid you are getting burned out. But … this notice in the bulletin is there. What should you do?

It is important to take an inventory occasionally to see where your time is spent during a week. How much time do you spend alone with your husband, enjoying and strengthening that relationship? How much time do you spend with your kids that doesn't include screens of any kind? Do you get outside, or are you usually in your office planning or preparing for things at your church? Are you constantly texting or on the phone? Are you able to be involved in your kids' school? Do you take time to relax and spend quiet time with the Lord or with friends on a purely social level? How balanced is your life?

There are thousands of good Bible studies out there, where we can "take in the Word," but my question is are we just taking in and piling up biblical knowledge for ourselves? Do we see personal and spiritual growth in ourselves, or "just something we have done for years"? Our pastor shared a quote from a seminary professor that puts this into perspective: "Lord, help my spiritual 'I dos' be bigger than my spiritual IQ." Think on that a bit and see where you are.

Now, you may not be overly involved in your church at all. You may have become one who lets everyone else serve you and the congregation, and you have become sort of a taker. Where do you contribute to your church family? We are all busy, and as my mom used to often say, "Many hands make light work." I remember one pastor in Houston, Texas, exhorting his congregation by saying, in his thick southern drawl, "If you are a member or a regular attender of your church, it is important to give at least one hour per week to serve here. Don't be a taker."

Many of us were raised with feelings of guilt and obligation, and we carry that into our adult life in most areas, including our religious life. Another thing that can affect us is if we never felt we were good enough and felt like we were on the outside looking in. We may feel that if we don't meet what we think others' expectations are, or that they won't like us, we will become a "church outsider." Does that sound healthy to you? It feels good to have other people think well of us and include us now, doesn't it? However, that may be another motivation for getting overly involved. Some religions actually build their worth and good standing with God on their good works! Doesn't sound like unconditional love, does it?

So you feel like you have to go to every single service, serve a certain amount of hours on a certain amount of committees, wear a certain type of clothes, volunteer for church events, sing in the choir, etc. We put so much pressure on ourselves sometimes, don't we?

On the surface, it might be that you just love to serve the Lord, or "they need my help," but it could be a lot deeper than that. Maybe you are trying to fill a void and earn points with God and others, so it could be more about you than it is about Him. Does that make sense as you look deeper?

Another issue that may come into play with the amount of time you volunteer is that maybe your marriage or home life is not the best. Maybe there is tension between your family members, chaos or drama, or any number of other things. I have always believed that we should feel our best in our own home, but when we don't, sometimes we will go somewhere else to find satisfaction, and where we get accolades and recognition. Are we serving God or human beings, or maybe both? God knows our hearts and the motivation behind our actions.

> Man looks on the outward appearance, but God looks on the heart. (1 Samuel 16:7)

> Serve wholeheartedly, as if you were serving the Lord, not men, because you know that the Lord will reward everyone for whatever good he does, whether slave or free. (Ephesians 6:7)

That includes you, lady in the practical pumps!

I don't see anything in that verse that says the Lord will stop loving or blessing us if we don't do as much as someone else. Remember, His love, forgiveness, and acceptance is *not* performance-based; nor is it something to compare with others.

I will also say that there is absolutely no room in ministry (or marriage) for competition. If you are trying to win, you are purposely trying to make the other person or ministry the loser, and that allows the enemy to damage unity.

Truth—"If you just sat there and breathed, He would love you just the same!" Read that again. God doesn't have favorites; nor does He keep score by way of our past sins. There is equal value and love for all of His children, including you!

So what does it mean in the verse above (Ephesians 6:7) when it says serve "wholeheartedly"? The definition of wholeheartedly is "to be fully or completely sincere, enthusiastic, energetic, hearty and earnest." Now how can we serve wholeheartedly when we are overworked and overcommitted, and our priorities are out of whack? Maybe your practical pumps are tightening and preventing you from walking freely. This might be a good time to evaluate what you are doing to serve *the Lord*— the balance of that with your family life, and if there needs to be an adjustment, by considering the following:

- Explore how you truly feel about serving.
- Are you feeling depleted, resentful, or taken advantage of?
- Do you feel you are serving outside of your gifting that has become a struggle for you?
- Are you frustrated with all the committee meetings and events while your family lives at home without you most of the time?
- Or are you serving in pure joy and freedom, filled with purpose?

How are your priorities? Are they God first, marriage and family second, and ministry third, or have they gotten mixed up and muddled? Practical pumps can give you stability, but the sides of the heels wear down, and the soles deteriorate, making walking in them painful and tiring for your entire body. Balance your practical pumps, or take them off, girl!

Could it be that it is time for a resole (resoul) of your practical pumps?

- Are you serving to please Him or serving to please others or yourself?
- Are you missing the joy of just being His daughter and communing with Him?
- Is your relationship with Him vibrant and growing or worn out?

If you can find balance, you will be able to serve with much greater joy. You know, God *will* provide someone else He has called to take up some of your duties, and *they* can be blessed by serving within *their* giftedness. Think about that. We are not indispensible in the Body of Christ.

Wouldn't it be a shame if we were holding onto some position or job in the church that we have always done and missed out on what God was calling us to do next? We are actually stopping Him from using us and someone else for His perfect purpose and plan. We need to step out of the practical pumps, let go and let *Him* lead and guide. Sound good?

It can be wonderful to walk with a steady stride in practical pumps, if we are walking in confidence and freedom. This could be the day you "resoul" your pumps for a new day and walk with greater joy.

> And this is love: that we walk in obedience to His commands. As you have heard from the beginning, His command is that you walk in love. (2 John 6)
>
> Those who walk uprightly enter into peace. (Isaiah 57:2)
>
> Your Word is a lamp unto my feet and a light unto my path. (Psalm 119:105)

Note: We may need to learn to follow Him and not run ahead of Him.

> And what does the Lord require of you? To act justly and to love mercy and walk humbly with your God. (Micah 6:8)

Practical pump faith can give you support and guidelines, but it can stifle your sweet relationship with Jesus and make it one of rules, rituals, obligations, and confinement. It can also mask the Holy Spirit's voice.

> Now the Lord is the Spirit and where the Spirit of the Lord is, there is freedom. (2 Corinthians 3:17)

The freedom that verse is talking about is the freedom to be who God made you to be and not what your past has told you. You are who God made you to be—nothing more and nothing less. Period. You have been given gifts and talents that are uniquely yours to be used with excellence as you serve Him.

So, slip those practical pumps on, polish them, make sure the tips and soles are strong, and serve the Lord with balance and godly purpose. Don't forget, however, to take them off sometimes, sit in His presence, seek a deeper walk with Him, and also make the time to enjoy other areas of your life with those you love.

Chapter 5
Standing on the Rock in Heels

Do you remember the old hymn, "Standing on the Promises"? The lyrics go like this:

> Standing on the promises of Christ my King
> Through eternal ages let His praises ring
> Glory in the highest I will shout and sing
> Standing on the promises of God.
> Standing, standing, standing on the promises of Christ, my Savior
> Standing, standing, I'm standing on the promises of God.

Whenever I sing this song, I think about standing strong, in the name of Jesus—standing on His Word as a strong and confident woman of God. I can picture my father's congregation standing up and singing this hymn with loud conviction, back in the day.

How old were you when you first put on your mother's heels and tried to walk in them? Were you a little girl of five years old, or was it when you were in middle school? Maybe your mom didn't wear heels, so you had to wait to wear them for your first prom or special occasion.

I remember trying to walk in my mom's heels when I was a little girl. My sisters and I would play dress up, fix each other's hair, put on pretty clothes with ruffles, and then strut our stuff around the house. I have precious memories of going to our grandmother's house in Seattle for family events and celebrations. As soon as we arrived, we would hug our grandparents, and then we kids would head downstairs to the basement where our grandma would have tons of stuff she brought home from her job at a thrift store. We girl cousins would all play dress up, make pretend meals with the old kitchen utensils and play food, and tend to our dolls, while the boys would play with army figures and put on helmets and pretend they were in a war. Oh, the days of imagination and healthy family gatherings ...how I miss them! I will never forget all the girl cousins wobbling up the stairs in old scuffed high heels. We thought we were so glamorous in our stilettos!

The term "stiletto" was named after the stiletto dagger and some of the first ones were from the nineteenth century, believe it or not. The first known designer of stilettos was Andre Perugia in 1906.

Even though the stilettos were more about sexiness for years, their most refined shape came in the early 1960s, as the shoe toes became longer and more pointed. If you are older like me, you may remember the first Barbie dolls with those little black stilettos. The popularity of high heels faded with the Beatle era but has resurfaced in recent years. We don't see a lot of them in our area, but we often see them on TV awards shows and in other urban areas in our travels.

Have you seen those poor teen girls dressed for their prom these days and how they look like new little fawns trying to walk? It is just so much fun to watch them walk in or out of a restaurant, and it really catches my eye when they all head to the women's restroom hanging onto one another! It is kind of a rite of passage for them in our society, isn't it? I always wonder how long it is before they take those heels off to dance at the prom.

Just like those teen girls in heels, that is what it's like when we first become believers, isn't it? We are wobbly, unsure, need help, and we are afraid to fall. More on that later.

The disadvantage to wearing stiletto heels often is that they can create skeletal and muscular problems, as well as cause pain by merely walking in them! Ask my sister, who wore them for years! They push the hips back, the bottom out, and put three times your weight on the balls of your feet (yikes!). I have to ask the question ... Did men or women invent these shoes? Hmm.

Stilettos are unstable on surfaces such as grass, sand, or uneven ground. Even worn on strong surfaces, women can fall. I remember Facebook videos of runway models falling off a pair of stilettos in front of cameras. Not good for their careers or their ankles, that's for sure!

What makes stilettos stand strong is a metal shaft imbedded in the heel and down the sole. Weaker materials or smaller straps require a wider heel, however, even though they are not quite as feminine looking.

Looking at the disadvantages and advantages of these beauties can help us translate them into our spiritual walk with Jesus and how we can be "standing on the rock in heels."

Let's look at the negatives first. Just like our spiritual walk can be unstable when we are not paying attention or watching what is ahead of us, we can fall in our walk with Jesus. Maybe we fall back into old habits or patterns. Maybe we begin to watch movies, visit computer sites, or read books that turn our minds in ungodly directions, or we spend more time with ungodly people, who can turn us away from God and do things that offend Him. Maybe we walk into a relationship we know is not righteous. Maybe we are having trouble in our marriages and another man pays more attention to us than our own husbands.

Maybe we are living with a guy, and we are aware of what God says about that, but we ignore it. "I am just human, and He understands. He will forgive me." Oh, we use all kinds of reasons to live with someone who we are not married to. Here are a few.

1. It's cheaper to live together instead of in two homes.
2. We have both been divorced, and we don't want to go through that again!
3. My guy doesn't want to get married, but I know he loves me.
4. We don't want to have a long-distance relationship.
5. We have to stay close to my ex's house because he is required by law to stay close to where their kids are. He really helps me with my kids, and I feel safer when we are living together.

Do you see how easy it is to justify our disobedience to the Lord God? "But, God ..." Ladies, this is a quick way to fall off of those spiritual stilettos! God cannot fully bless us if we are truly defying Him by disobedience.

When we continue to purposely sin against God, before we know it, our walk with God is interrupted, and we get distracted by other activities or by our own personal struggles or trauma. We take our eyes off of the Lord and try to do it ourselves. Plop! There we go to the ground and experience more pain.

"Why does God keep putting me through all of this?!" "Why does He allow bad things to happen to me?" Guess what? That trauma, breakup, crisis, etc. wasn't even about Him. It is our own rebellion, our refusal to follow His Word, and maybe how we ignore Him that keeps us wobbling in our heels. Many times we pick and choose which parts of the Bible we will believe and obey. It is impossible to walk on a fence with stilettos, ladies! Think about that a bit.

> So, I say, live by the Spirit, and you will not gratify the desires of the sinful nature. For the sinful nature desires what is contrary to the Spirit, and the Spirit what is contrary to the sinful nature. They are in conflict with each other, so that you do not do what you want. (Galatians 5:16–17)

Sometimes our past catches up with us, and we define ourselves by it instead of defining ourselves by who God says we are. This is a horrible trap of the enemy.

There is an important concept that explains how we can let this happen. It is called "looking out of the windshield instead of the rearview mirror."

"If you were driving and all you did was look out the rearview mirror, you could bump into things, run off the road, or could be fatally injured. If you just looked out of the windshield and never checked your rearview mirror, you might be hit from behind and not see a potential danger approaching.

"The same thing goes for our lives. If we just look at our past and live in its issues, we cannot move forward in safety and strength. If we only look forward but not remember what was before, we could fall back into the same traps and patterns we were in. The past needs to be dealt with, but not completely forgotten. It is part of who we are, but it doesn't have to have power over us or define us as we drive away from it." (*Chained No More*, by Robyn Besemann, WestBow Press)

The enemy will use whatever he can to keep us from living the life God would have us live. That is his self-proclaimed number one priority for God's children. Remember Adam and Eve? What the enemy keeps forgetting, however, is that God is bigger than he is. We can step over Satan in our spiritual stilettos every single time.

God is omniscient (knows everything), is omnipresent (is everywhere), and is omnipotent (all powerful). He knows everything about us from the moment of conception to the day we die. It's hard for us to comprehend sometimes when we forget where we put our keys on any given day, right? He is the Almighty God and He loves *you*, just for who He created you to be. Believe it!

"His eyes are on the ways of mortals. He sees their every step" (Job 34:21) This means He sees us and knows us no matter what type of spiritual shoes we are wearing!

"The Lord searches every heart and understands every motive behind the thoughts. If you seek Him, He will be found by you; but if you forsake Him, He will reject you forever" (1 Chronicles 28:9. Honestly, this verse has always made me feel uncomfortable because it says He knows the motive behind my thoughts. Are you kidding me?! Sometimes, I don't even know that!

In our world today, there are no absolutes, rules, and regulations— just suggestions and everyone's "truth" is okay. Well, God's Truth is absolute. You can count on it. It is like my dad used to say from a quote, "God said it; I believe it; that settles it."

There are times when we walk on uneven ground in life. When I was the camp mom at our church camp, Camp Harlow, there was a lot of uneven ground on the property. There were very few paved areas, lots of uneven lawns, and many things to trip over, including the big roots of massive fir trees. I was always tripping over something, especially when I was paying attention to kids and not looking ahead. I would trip over pine cones, rocks, branches, and backpacks. You name it, and I tripped over it. I never really got injured, but it was annoying.

Nowadays, I walk slower, watch where I am going, check for cracks in the sidewalk, rocks waiting to trip me up, and anything that looks like a trap, as I put it. How about you? I mean, I don't want to break a hip. I have things to do!

There is also a lot of spiritually uneven ground, isn't there? Many things can trip us up as we try to walk steady with Jesus. Here are several "rocks" that can send us spinning out of control or drop us to the ground in our spiritual heels.

- Not spending time in God's Word and listening for the Holy Spirit's voice and guidance.
- Not connecting and communing with Him in prayer or joining others for growth and fellowship for support and encouragement.
- Letting others pull us away from our beliefs and values. This would include spouses and extended family members. We will stand alone before the throne on Judgment Day, ladies.
- Letting our priorities change because of other activities. Many times, we give God the bottom spot on our priority list.
- Living in willful, sinful habits or actions. We know what they are but can ignore them.

My commitment to myself is that "if it offends my God, it needs to offend me." What is in your life right now that would offend your God? Do you care about that? If we want God's best for us and to be our best, we may need to realign our spiritual heels and walk forward in a strong stride—not one that falters to the left or to the right.

For a while, we can be walking hand in hand with Jesus and then, before we know it, we are stepping out of fellowship. That's when we can trip and fall in those spiritual high heels. Sometimes, we can even lose our way, take off our stilettos and slip on our spiritual flip-flops or slippers, and follow a path of bumps, bruises, and falls—many times leaving deep scars. Without paying attention to the Holy Spirit's guidance, we are trying to "do it on our own" and can miss many opportunities and lessons for growth. Our walk is no longer stable. We don't "hear His voice." We are, in essence, walking precariously on uneven ground in the dark.

So how do we walk more securely in our new spiritual stilettos? We can fill up our lives with self-help Christian books, magazines, websites, and Christian TV, but are we growing and putting feet to what we are learning? Do we let everyone else do the exploring of His Word, or are we taking that walk ourselves?

Here in America, we can become starstruck with celebrities, whether they are movie or TV stars, athletes, politicians, or even celebrity evangelists, speakers, and pastors. There are huge conferences, television shows, DVD series, books, and church events, and we just can't seem to get enough of her or him. There are endless products to help us proclaim the name of Jesus, but what if there weren't all these people and products and resources—only us and God's Word? Would that be enough?

I have heard many people rely on "secondhand Christianity," which is the feeling we can be grandfathered in, so to speak, because maybe our parents or our spouse are strong in their faith. Remember, we will stand before the throne alone, friend. Here on earth, we answer *only* for ourselves—our words, actions, decisions, and attitudes. We cannot let our spouse or our kids or anyone else determine if we go to church or not, if we have devotions or not, or if we pray or not. We allow ourselves to be pressured into doing things that could be against God and keep us from having a close relationship with Him. We don't answer for something our spouse or parent or kids say to us, but we will surely answer to God for what we do and say in reaction. It is hard to take that in sometimes because first reactions can be swift.

> Consider it pure joy, my brothers, whenever you face trials of many kinds, because you know that the testing of your faith develops perseverance. Perseverance must finish its work so that you may be mature and complete, not lacking anything. If any of you lacks wisdom, he should ask God, who gives generously to all without finding fault, and it will be given to him. But when he asks, he must believe and not doubt, because he who doubts is like a wave of the sea, blown and tossed by the wind. That man should not think he will receive anything from the Lord; he is a double-minded man, unstable in all he does. (James 1:2–8)

When we are truly "standing on the rock in heels," we make Jesus Christ that strong metal shank, embedded in our heart and soul, and stabilizing our heels so we can have strength in our walk with Him. Anything less is weaker and doesn't stand on its own.

What are some things that can weaken us in our walk with Jesus? Looking around us these days, there are many. I mentioned many of them in regard to what can put us on uneven ground, but let's add a few more things to think about and the effects they have on us.

- What websites do you explore and connect with? Would you mind if God Himself was looking at them with you? He is.
- Do you get caught up in romance novels that keep you looking at your own husband as not as attentive or romantic?
- What does your social media footprint look like? Do you represent God well? Would your Facebook or Instagram friends see that you are a woman of faith and integrity, or would they be surprised?
- If you are addicted to video games, are they games that would honor the Lord?
- Does social media suck the hours out of your day, so that you don't get more productive things done? Maybe it is your way to block out what you are living right now. Don't let these addictions replace the healing of the Lord God in your life. His healing lasts. Gaming and social media are merely temporary fixes.

We get to decide how we will live our lives and how strongly we stand on the Rock. We cannot blame our upbringing, what others are doing, what is expected of us by other flawed human beings, or anything else. Look deep. Look deeper with honesty.

It is easy for us to find fault with others and deflect away from our own issues. For those of us who feel we have the spiritual gift of judging others, it is time to step off those ugly high heels! It's time to look at our own spiritual footwear before we fall flat on our faces. We certainly don't like others to judge or condemn us, do we? We don't know what someone has lived, if he or she ever walked into a church, or the damage that has led the person to our churches. God knows everything about all of us, and

He needs to be the One to bring us to Himself. We, as His children, are to extend the arms of Jesus, and let Him do His own business with others.

> Why do you look down on your brother? For we will all stand before God's judgment seat. It is written: "As surely as I live," says the Lord, "every knee will bow before Me; every tongue will confess to God. So then, each of us will give an account of himself (or herself) to God. (Romans 14:10–12)

Each of us is on our own walk with God, wearing whatever spiritual shoes we have on. We will all trip and fall sometimes but will hopefully get back up, and He will lead us to walk on higher ground. Our prayer support and encouragement for each other is our job and our responsibility, as sisters in the Lord. Let God do His own business, and let's concentrate on our own walk with Him.

Now that we are focused on our own walk, imagine what it looks like to begin "standing on the rock in heels" with confidence. It means:

- Stand up straight, shoulders back, with our chin up and looking straight ahead as we follow the Lord God with every step. There should not be bad spiritual posture but confidence.
- That with God, all things are possible, to those who follow Him.
- We reach higher and higher as we grow strong and assured in who we are in Jesus Christ.
- Our spiritual core is the rod of Christ down the center of us, and nothing will be able to knock us over. Nothing.

> I have set the Lord always before me because He is at my right hand. I will not be shaken. (Psalm 16:8)

What are the steps you need to take to walk boldly and confidently in your spiritual stilettos? Please carefully and prayerfully consider the following:

- What will it specifically take to get you there?
- What do you need to get rid of in your life?

- What do you need to adjust?
- What do you need to do to grow in His grace and freedom?
- What is holding you back?

Are you willing to take those steps? Like gorgeous sparkly stilettos, it may be wobbly at first, and you may be afraid of falling, but trust Him to take you step by step, if you are *truly* willing. One of the most beautiful things about the Lord is that no matter how many times we fall or walk away, He is there, and His arms are open to help us stand up again. His love never fails!

> He who dwells in the shelter of the Most High will rest in the shadow of the Almighty. I will say of the Lord, "He is my refuge and my fortress, my God, whom I trust." (Psalm 91:1–2)

Now, just because we put on those spiritual stilettos and have a resolve to walk strongly, it doesn't mean we can't step into the mud or trip on a rock, and things can get slippery for a bit. We may go through a marital crisis, loss of a loved one, loss of a job, or heavy health issues. When we are truly "standing on the rock in heels," we can walk with stable strides and hold onto the Almighty God when we might begin to wobble.

God gave us promises to give us strength. They are:

- "I will never leave you nor forsake you" (Hebrews 13:5).
- "Behold I am with you even to the end of the age" (Matthew 28:20).
- "In all your ways, acknowledge Him and He will direct your path" (Proverbs 3:6)
- "Thy Word is a Lamp unto my feet and a Light unto my path" (Psalm 119:105).

Now there is the metal shank of Christ we have been talking about!

> So, be careful to do what the Lord your God has commanded you; do not turn aside to the right or to

the left. Walk in all the ways that the Lord your God has commanded you, so that you may live and prosper and prolong your days in the land that you will possess. (Deuteronomy 5:33)

Ladies, beginning today, choose to put on those gorgeous spiritual stilettos, kick the enemy out of the way, hold firm on the promises and truths of God's Word, fill yourself with Him, stay on the right path, and begin to live life to the fullest—"standing on the rock in heels." Get ready for the most wonderful walk of your life, full of blessings, confidence, and pure joy, as you take every stride as a strong woman of God, saved by grace and valued by God Himself. You look mahvelous!

Epilogue

I have always loved shoes. I enjoy shopping for them, trying them on, strutting my stuff around the store, and then deciding on the perfect pair to buy. Sometimes I shop for a specific shoe for a particular outfit or occasion, and sometimes I just like to wander through rack after rack to see what's out there. My husband said he expects me to come home from any shopping trip with girls with at least one pair of new shoes. Hey, don't judge me!

As I began the topic for this book and for speaking engagements, it all made sense to me. There are many more types of footwear that I could equate to our spiritual walk, and maybe there will be a sequel to this book. My mind is flooded with ideas, such as boots, waders, ballet shoes, flats, etc. Maybe someday …

I will ask you these questions one more time:

- Are you in baby shoes and just beginning your walk with God? Are you growing in Him or have you been merely staying a baby Christian?
- Are you in bunny slippers where your walk is complacent, lazy, and too comfortable?
- Are you in flip-flops and just barely living a walk with God today? Maybe you think asking Jesus into your heart is enough, with little or no relationship with Him at all.
- Are you in practical pumps and doing all you can to meet what you think are His requirements and list of dos and don'ts? Have your church involvements left you weary and resentful? Or are you walking strong in beautiful spiritual stilettos as a strong

woman of God, living free in His grace and love and always reaching for more, while walking in *His* stride?

It would be easy for me to tell you what you ought to do, but what are you going to do to step into those heels? This is *your* life! It is up to you and your desire to be all God made you to be, so you can walk in His confidence and joy.

Here are some practical ideas to set you up for a successful walk with God:

- Evaluate your personal walk with Jesus. Take your time and be honest.
- Find a Bible study (personal or small group) that will challenge you in the areas you struggle with. You can Google "women's Bible study" or call your church to connect with a small group.
- Find resources to help you find healing from the hurts and issues that keep you down.
- Check out *Chained No More: A Journey of Healing for Adult Children of Divorce/Childhood Brokenness* at amazon.com or www. robynbministries.com/chainednomore.
- Seek counsel or a mentor—someone who can guide you to a stronger walk in God's freedom.
- "Do the work to make it work." Don't merely keep praying about it; put feet to your prayers, and take one step at a time.
- Walk with no fear but with confidence in who He made you to be. If you don't know about that, get into His Word to find out and walk in it.
- Be strong and courageous, ladies. We have a mighty God who wants you to succeed. By the way, so do I!

"Standing on the rock in heels"? You can believe you can rock those spiritual heels because your Creator is the One showing you the way. Yes, you can!

Printed in the United States
By Bookmasters